DONAL NEARY SJ

Pilgrim in Lent

DAILY PRAYER IN LENT

D0104088

A Liturgical Press Book

THE LITURGICAL PRESS
Collegeville, Minnesota

First published 1992 by
THE COLUMBA PRESS
County Dublin, Ireland

Cover by Bill Bolger

The reflections in this book are taken from the following sources and the author and publisher gratefully acknowledge permission to use this copyright material.

David Adams, *The Edge of Glory,* Triangle; Wilkie Au SJ, *By Way of the Heart,* Paulist; L and C Boff, *Introducing Liberation Theology,* Burns and Oates; Eamonn Bredin, *Disturbing the Peace,* Columba; Sheila Cassidy, *Audacity To Believe,* Fount; *Good Friday People,* Darton, Longman and Todd; Donal Dorr, *The Social Justice Agenda,* Gill and Macmillan; Segundo Galilea, *The Beatitudes,* Gill and Macmillan; B Grogan/U O'Connor, *Love Beyond All Telling,* Irish Messenger; Gerard W Hughes SJ, *God of Surprises; Walk to Jerusalem,* Darton, Longman and Todd; Brendan Kennelly, *Voices,* Blackstaff Press; Dermot Lane, *Christ at the Centre,* Veritas; Enda McDonagh, *The Small Hours of Belief,* Columba; Albert Nolan, *God in South Africa,* CCII; Donal O'Leary, *Creative Crisis,* Columba; Joan Puls OSF, *A Spirituality of Compassion,* XX111rd Publications; Br Roger of Taize, *No Greater Love; His Love is a Fire,* Chapman; Ronald Rolheiser, *Forgotten Among the Lilies, The Restless Heart,* Spire; Terry Tastard, *The Spark in the Soul,* Darton, Longman and Todd.We acknowledge our thanks also to *Intercom* (quote from Melvyn Mullins), *The Catholic Herald* (quotes from Ronald Rolheiser), *The Tablet* (quotes from Sheila Cassidy and Patrick Barry), and *The Sacred Heart Messenger* (quote from John Sweeney). Unacknowledged reflections are by the author.

ISBN 0-8146-2123-6

Contents

Preface

This is what the Lord wants of you:
to act justly,
love tenderly,
and walk humbly with your God.

These words of Amos are a sort of backdrop or slogan to a spirituality for Lent. This spirituality or way of praying in Lent could be said to flow from this understanding of God's word for us: it is a way of life balanced between prayer ('walking humbly with God'), relationships and friendships ('loving tenderly') and love of the wider community of people and the world ('acting justly').

Lent is a call to conversion in our lives: the themes of *Pilgrim in Lent* offer an opportunity and a challenge to view the directions of our life (week 1), the true glory of Jesus (week 2), religion (week 3), life through the eye of faith (week 4), life and death (week 5) and Holy Week in the all-embracing context of the death and resurrection of Jesus.

Pilgrim in Lent, with use of Scripture suitable for the season, gives a prayerful integration of these three movements of Lenten spirituality with material for reflection or prayer for each day. The Sunday gospels of the Lectionary form a basis for each week's Scripture. Links are indicated between these and the christian life, especially with reference to the paschal mystery.

Lent is a time of renewal of the love of God in each of us, and of conversion to live out of this experience of Jesus Christ in love of others. The scripture selections, meditations and reflections in *Pilgrim in Lent* give a gentle and consistent invitation to allow God's love in the death and resurrection of Jesus into our lives, and to let that love change us, so that 'we put on the mind of Christ'.

How to use Pilgrim in Lent

You may use *Pilgrim in Lent* for personal prayer. It may be read slowly: there is no hurry to cover all the material. The meditations and reflections enlighten some of the meaning of the Scripture.

It is best to find a time and a place when you will be least disturbed for prayer. For the beginning of prayer, some of these hints may be helpful:

Choose a place and a time for prayer. Find a posture for prayer which suits you: some like to sit, others to lie down, others to kneel, others to walk slowly out of doors. Begin with a few minutes of quiet: either a quietening exercise like listening to whatever sounds you can hear, or attending to the rhythm of your breathing. You might listen to a few minutes of taped music, or light a candle and let its flame bring you into the atmosphere of prayer.

Read the Scripture slowly; read it again, pausing where you find it holds you. If you are praying alone, you might read the Scripture aloud. Stay with whatever phrase or words of the Scripture strike you; let them echo in your mind, or talk to the Lord, sharing what's in your heart with him.

The meditation can be a help to drawing some meaning from the Scripture. You may not need to use the meditations at your time of prayer, as you may talk to God simply in your own words. In a time of dryness or distraction, the meditation can be your personal prayer or a start to it.

The reflections, usually taken from a modern spiritual writer, link the paschal mystery with some aspect of faith or life today. Like any spiritual reading, these reflections feed our prayer.

Prayer material is given for six days, except in the first and last weeks. On the seventh day you could return to some prayer-material which you found helpful in your prayer; repetition of Scripture deepens our prayer and our appreciation of the mystery of Jesus.

Pilgrim in Lent may also be used for prayer services during Lent. With the addition of some intercessory prayers, for example, or some taped music or hymns, the material for each day suits community prayer, school assemblies, prayer sessions during retreats and non-Eucharistic liturgies.

A commitment to praying the mystery of Jesus' death and resurrection during Lent deepens the love of God in a person's life, and can give hope and encouragement in the struggles of life. It involves us in the vision of hope, the horizon of faith and the light of love which is the gift of God in Jesus Christ. Prayer does good for the person who prays, and does good for those whose lives are touched by a person who prays. For in prayer, we pray not only from ourselves but from the Spirit of God, who prays within each of us and who was sent into the world from the moment when Jesus breathed his life to God for the sake of the world.

Donal Neary SJ

Introduction The six weeks of Lent lead us into the good and evil desires of our hearts in the invitation of God in Jesus Christ to deepen our relationship with God, and to become more involved in our christian life. Though we want to be people of the gospel and of Christ, we know also the tugs in the opposite directions.

Scripture The 'greatest commandment' of Jesus is a suitable encouragement at the beginning of Lent.

When the Pharisees heard that he had silenced the Sadducees they got together, and to put him to the test, one of them put a further question, 'Master, which is the greatest command-ment of the Law?' Jesus said to him, 'You must love the Lord your God with all your heart, with all your soul and with all your mind. This is the greatest and the first commandment. The second resembles it: 'You must love your neighbour as yourself. On these two commandments hang the whole Law and the Prophets too.
Matthew 22: 34-40.

Other Scripture The following of Christ is a mystery for this life and the next; our faith, hope and love are often tested 'like gold in the fire' by opposing attractions of life.
1 Peter 1: 6-9.

Meditation
Today is the beginning of a journey
which will recall to us
the deepest experiences of human life:

a six week's pilgrimage on the paths
of resurrection's victory over death,
love's victory over injustice,
healing's victory over pain.

This is the paschal path;
and Jesus is the way
to find direction on our own paschal path:
to connect ourselves step by step
with the truth of what it means to be human
and to be christian.

Begin again:
Begin again to pray in your heart.
Begin again to the call of friendship.
Begin again to the knowledge that pain is part of life.
Begin again to the sure hope of risen life.

Begin again to walk with Jesus;
to be led on your path of your life:

Begin in faith, hope and love.

Lord, I offer you these weeks of Lent;
may I know you, love you and serve you more.

Reflection The Beginning of Healing

That mixed company of believers and half-believers who come to pray in a crisis may not be the perfect limbs of Paul's vision of the body of Christ. Perhaps they form the handicapped body of Christ and their prayer the beginning of their healing. Their prayer may seem selfish and slight; but even slight and selfish prayer may be a beginning; it can open the spiritually handicapped and inadequate (that is all of us) to Christ's healing. It refers us to him as to our healer. It opens our hearts to the Father of all mankind. It is never the end of the story, but it may be a much better beginning than appears at first.

Patrick Barry OSB, in *The Tablet*.

Thursday after Ash Wednesday **Looking Ahead**

Introduction The end of our Lenten journey is certain: the path is known. Through death and suffering, Jesus will rise in glory. The way we each share that journey is different.

Scripture Allow the mystery of Jesus' prophecy of his own death and resurrection touch your heart. You may be unbelieving like some of the disciples, or want it to be different. We pray for trust to follow him like this.

Then taking the Twelve aside he said to them, 'Look, we are going up to Jerusalem, and everything that is written by the Prophets about the Son of man is to come true. For he will be handed over to the gentiles and will be mocked, maltreated and spat on, and when they have scourged him they will put him to death; and on the third day he will rise again.' But they could make nothing of this; what he said was quite obscure to them; they did not understand what he was telling them.
Luke 18: 31-34.

Other Scripture The prayer Jesus prayed on the Cross refers to the suffering he would go through; at the end he prays in thanks to God for the victory he knows God will bring about.
Psalm 22.

Meditation
Jesus told them he would
suffer and be killed
and then would rise from the dead.

A plunge into the mystery of being human:
the mystery of pain, weakness and death,
the mystery of failure and of fragility,
the mystery of injustice and of greed,
the mystery of following the path known to be right.

10

This is the paschal mystery:
a religious name
for the mystery in our lives
of suffering, of death, of pain,

of faith that is strengthened in struggle,
of hope that never dies
and of love that doesn't fail.

Please, God, let me know the paschal vision,
let me feel and live in the light of your vision,
the vision of hope and of love
which is the death and resurrection of Jesus.

Reflection The Way Ahead

One day you understood that, without your being aware of it, a yes had already been inscribed in your innermost depths. And so you chose to go forward in the footsteps of Christ, a choice no one can make for another.

In silence in the presence of Christ, you heard him say, 'Come, follow me; I will give you a place to rest your heart.'

And so you are led to the audacity of a yes that lasts until your dying breath. This yes leaves you exposed. There is no other way.

Brother Roger of Taizé, *No Greater Love.*

Friday after Ash Wednesday Denying Yourself

Introduction Denying yourself something has long been associated with Lent: of itself it is not necessarily pleasing to God. It must be linked with some outreach to others and to prayer. Similarly with anything else 'we do for Lent'.

Scripture The realistic words of Jesus about bearing one's cross give encouragement in the struggles and sufferings of our life. They recall to us the paschal truth that life comes from death.

Jesus said to his disciples, 'If anyone wants to be a follower of mine, let him renounce himself and take up his cross and follow me. Anyone who wants to save his life will lose it; but anyone who loses his life for my sake will find it. What, then, will anyone gain by winning the whole world and forfeiting his life? Or what can anyone offer in exchange for his life?' *Matthew 16: 24-26.*

Other Scripture Faith draws us out to the needs of others. *James 2: 14-17.*

Meditation
Giving up something for Lent,
can seem so futile
when I remember
some of the starvation I've seen:

On a bus journey through India one night
when we made one of our stops,
I threw away a rotten banana.
I looked back and noticed that
three men immediately ran to the bin
and fought over the rotten banana.

When I think of fasting
I think of them,
three hungry men in the starry Indian night,
fighting over my garbage.

12

I think of the millions who have no choice but to fast;
of the millions who are thirsty
not because they gave up drink
but because we seem to have given up on them.

It might even put me off fasting;
what use is my fast –
except to slim a fat body –
unless another benefits from what I give up?

As I fast – whatever it may be –
may I always remember it is but a gesture,
a gesture which reminds me that
others fast through no choice of their own,
and that Jesus is hungry in them.

Lord, open my heart
to all who are needy
in our world of plenty.

Reflection Inequality

The mere fact that some people are more wealthy than others is not, in itself, a social injustice. But the existence of gross poverty alongside conspicuous wealth is morally unacceptable. The fact that in our world millions of people do not have the basic necessities of life while others live in luxury is a basic injustice: it infringes the most fundamental human right of all - the right to life. The christian tradition maintains that the goods of the earth are there for the welfare of all the earth's inhabitants – and that the right to private property takes second place to this.

Donal Dorr, *The Social Justice Agenda*

Introduction An essential 'way' of Lent is prayer. Renewal of christian life includes always the practice of prayer.

Scripture Prayer is not only our own effort: it is our joining in with the prayer of Jesus Christ. He is praying for us now in his risen life; we join our prayer with his.

I pray not only for these
but also for those
who through their teaching will come to believe in me.
John 17: 20.

Other Scripture This poem includes many of the essentials of christian prayer: need, trust, sorrow, petition, gratitude, help-lessness.
Psalm 86.

Meditation
A man of God once dreamed he saw a ladder stretching between heaven and earth:
God's angels were going up and down.

Who are God's angels for me?
Who is on God's ladder for me?

The child with the smile of the innocent,
the bird singing with all its heart,
the friend with the advice or consolation,
the spouse and the commitments and acts of love;
'God's ladder' is peopled and crowded
with the people and things that lead me to God
and enlighten my faith.

Also on my 'God's ladder' –
the people who hurt me,
those who cheated me,
illness and sickness,

fears and anxieties
all are angels, messengers of God.

In his dream, Jacob saw God standing beside him:
the ladder was God's way of showing him
that he was present to him all the time.

Prayer is finding God all the time:

Lord, help me to find you in all of my life.

Reflection God really is our teacher ...

...and he alone can teach us to pray, or rather, he alone prays in us...If in prayer you find yourself constantly asking yourself, 'Am I praying the right way?', that is an indication that you are allowing yourself to be controlled and dominated by other peoples' suggestions. God wants to share with you in the unique being he has given you: he does not want you to approach him as though he can only respond to set words prescribed by those who know. We have to learn to trust our own experience, our richest source of knowledge. We must listen to others who can help us read and interpret our own experience, but we must not allow them so to dominate our thinking that we ignore our own inner promptings, for to do so is to renounce our freedom and 'to lose our very selves'.

Gerard W Hughes SJ, *God of Surprises*.